YEARS 5/6

ENGL SH
S ARPE ER:
Spelling

J H Rice

KEY ENGLISH SKILLS
FOR

CW00460371

Introduction

Poor spelling can have a disquieting effect on the reader. In many it merely provokes a concern as to the reliability and authority of the writer; in others it rouses a level of pedantry and frustration that is out of all proportion to the importance of the text. Certainly, spelling matters – the more influential the writer, the greater is the blunder of a typographical error or misplaced homophone.

Edward Carney (1994: 79) states, 'Spelling errors have social penalties. If you cannot spell you are thought to be uneducated and, by a further savage twist, unintelligent.'

It is difficult to determine at what age and at what level of authority poor spelling engenders such negative associations. My favourite misspelling is from a six-year-old who sent a Christmas card to 'Mr Rice and your Secret tart' – after some amusement in the staffroom it became apparent that she had attempted to write 'secretary'. Another favourite was from an undergraduate. It read, 'Samuel's closet (closest) relationship is with his mother', which should serve as a warning to those who rely on automatic spell-checkers. The unintended humour of these misspellings is entertaining, the consequence minimal.

Contrast these examples with the government's withdrawal and reprinting of 48,000 KS2 spelling posters in 2000 due to typographical errors. It drew the headline, 'Shame over spelling blunder' from the normally reserved BBC. Correct spelling is important if you need your message to be taken seriously.

For many children, spelling isn't easy and those who are fortunate to have a good orthographic memory should perhaps reflect upon the following quote from Samuel Langhorne Clemens, better known as Mark Twain:

'I have had an aversion to good spelling for sixty years and more, merely for the reason that when I was a boy there was not a thing I could do creditably except spell according to the book. It was a poor and mean distinction and I early learned to disenjoy it. I suppose that this is because the ability to spell correctly is a talent, not an acquirement. There is some dignity about an acquirement, because it is a product of your own labor. It is wages earned, whereas to be able to do a thing merely by the grace of God and not by your own effort transfers the distinction to our heavenly home – where possibly it is a matter of pride and satisfaction but it leaves you naked and bankrupt.'

Mark Twain's Autobiography Volume II.

Of course, we know that spelling can be acquired otherwise a large number of people in the teaching profession would be wasting a huge amount of time. The flip side of this statement is that for some children (and adults) spelling is a skill that requires structure, support and much celebration of achievement.

The activities presented in this book are based on the appendices for the new draft National Curriculum for English. The resources are unashamedly worksheet based and these materials are intended to be used alongside, and in conjunction with, other teaching methods. The materials relate to the curriculum's spelling guidelines, which are given in the form of rules.

McLeod (1961) states that the value of a spelling rule can be assessed by reference to a number of criteria:

- it should apply to a large number of words;
- it must have few exceptions;
- it must be easy to state and understand;
- it must cover only appropriate words.

Rules offer the pupil an opportunity to spell a large number of words in exchange for a small amount of learning, but where the rule is complex and applies to limited examples its efficiency falters. In these cases, rote learning of individual words may be more time-effective for some children. Teachers, through their knowledge of pupils' learning styles, are best placed to judge the most appropriate method of teaching.

Using this book

Teacher's notes provide further information about spellings, contextualise the activities and offer suggestions for extension, as necessary.

The Activity sheets are described and explained beneath the Teacher's notes and are indicated by the banner shown on the left.

EXTENSION

Extension activities can be found in the right-hand column next to the relevant activity, beneath this Extension heading.

Resources

WORD FARM

Set deep in the countryside and hidden away behind these rusty old gates lies Word Farm. The owner of Word Farm is Chris. You can see him on the right.

Word Farm is the place where words are taken apart, recycled and put back together. This is dangerous work. Broken words leak letter radiation and the animals have become hyper-intelligent! This is good news for Chris because the animals help him with his work.

AROUND THE FARM

CONSTRUCTION SHED

Letter shack

This is where the chickens hang out.

Eggstein

Eggstein is an egg-straordinarily clever chicken and a proper egghead! He's in charge of the Chicken Picker Crew but he's always crowing on about something...

LETTER SHACK

Chicken Picker Crew

These birds are the real workers on the farm. They sort through the letters and words, choosing which ones need to go together. They're told what to do by Eggstein but he talks so much that they sometimes forget to listen! Who can blame them?

William

This horse is William. He pulls the heavy letters and words around between the workshops.

Construction shed

Bring your ear plugs because this is where all the action is. This is the home of...

... Baarbara and the Heavy Metal Gang

Baarbara, Martha and their gang are the flock who rock! They're the word wranglers. They find the best way to join letters by tying them together, stitching them up or welding them in place. They're great music fans, too, and love a bit of thrash metal! Can you see Baarbara? - she's the one wearing a welding mask!

Recycling barn

This is the place where words are chopped up ready to be reused, but it's also the training ground for ...

The Duck Squad

These ducks love to pull words apart and break them up into little lettery pieces. Working with chainsaws, sledgehammers or just their highly-trained wings, they can split up words for recycling. The true identity of the Ninja Duck is a mystery....

Rooter and Tooter

Rooter and Tooter root out words from all over the world. We'll leave it to you to guess which pig is which!

Terry and Crumb

The two silliest bulls on the farm. They're just too daft for most word work but they try hard to make the other animals smile!

Endings which sound like /shus/ spelt -cious or -tious

Rules and guidelines*

Endings which sound like /shus/ spelt -cious or -tious	Not many common words end like this. If the root word ends in -ce, the /sh/ sound is spelt as **c**, e.g. vice/vicious; grace/gracious; space/spacious; malice/malicious. **Exception:** anxious.	vicious, precious, conscious, delicious, malicious, suspicious, ambitious, cautious, fictitious, infectious, nutritious.

Additional information

The difficulty with the rule provided is that the child is likely to be presented with the /shus/ spelling and may find it difficult to trace back to find the root word. While 'spacious' is clearly related to the root word 'space', few pupils of this age would have the vocabulary to relate 'malicious' to 'malice' without guidance. Equally, some -cious words, e.g. delicious, ferocious and precious cannot be traced back in this way.

As an alternative (to which there are still exceptions) most words ending with -tious will have a corresponding noun that ends in -tion. So we have: ambitious (ambition); cautious (caution); fictitious (fiction); infectious (infection); nutritious (nutrition); repetitious (repetition); superstitious (superstition).

Exceptions: conscientious (conscience); pretentious (pretension).

The word 'suspicious' is the only (vocabulary appropriate) word that has a corresponding noun where the /shun/ ending is spelt -cion.

ACTIVITIES

Endings which sound like /shus/ spelt -cious or -tious (1)

This activity encourages pupils to relate -tious words to -tion. Pupils need to be made aware that this rule has exceptions, e.g. scrumptious.

Endings which sound like /shus/ spelt -cious or -tious (2)

This activity corresponds to the Rules and guidelines information. Children are guided to find the -ce root word and are then asked to find the meanings of these words.

EXTENSION

Pupils to look through their reading books for more examples of words with a /shus/ ending. How many of these words have a related /shun/ ending and how many do not?

Endings which sound like /shus/ spelt -cious or -tious (1)

Baarbara and the flock who rock have to add a /shus/ sound to these words.
The problem is that they don't know whether they should attach -tious or -cious!

Eggstein has some useful advice:

> *Try adding a /shun/ sound to the first part of the word. If it makes a real word, add -tious; if not, add -cious.*

Say:	Can the word have a -tion /shun/ ending?	✓ or ✗	Write:
ambi /shus/	ambi -tion	✓	ambitious
pre /shus/	pre -tion	✗	precious
gra /shus/			
vora /shus/			
supersti /shus/			
vi /shus/			
ficti /shus/			

Say:	Can the word have a -tion /shun/ ending?	✓ or ✗	Write:
nutri /shus/			
fero /shus/			
atro /shus/			
spa /shus/			
infec /shus/			
cau /shus/			
cons /shus/			

Clue: say con /shus/

> *That's some bodacious advice, Eggy!*

> *Be suspicious of the word suspicious! It's the only -cious word that can also have a /shun/ ending – suspicion and suspicion.*

© Badger Learning

7

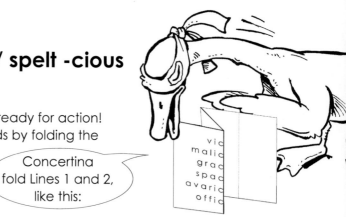

ACTIVITY

Endings which sound like /shus/ spelt -cious or -tious (2)

The ducks are back and they're mean, keen and ready for action! Help them to knock off the -ious part of these words by folding the paper and adding an e.

Concertina fold Lines 1 and 2, like this:

Line 1	Line 2	Line 3

v i c i o u s

m a l i c i o u s

g r a c i o u s

s p a c i o u s

a v a r i c i o u s

o f f i c i o u s

Write the new words and their meanings below:

_____

_____

Do you know what all of these words mean? Take a look in a book!

_____

_____

_____

_____

_____

Endings which sound like /shul/

Rules and guidelines*

Endings which sound like /shul/	**-cial** is common after a vowel and **-tial** after a consonant, but there are some exceptions. **Exceptions:** initial, financial, commercial, provincial (though the spelling of the last three could be said to come from finance, commerce and province).	official, special, artificial, partial, confidential, essential.

Additional information

As can be seen from the table below, a sufficient number of /shul/ words follow the consonant/vowel rule for it to be a useful teaching device, particularly within the constraints of vocabulary expectation. The exceptions to this rule (initial, financial, commercial and provincial) can be taught as a separate list.

	-cial	-tial
/shul/ after a vowel	artificial beneficial crucial facial glacial official racial social (and antisocial) special	initial
/shul/ after a consonant	financial commercial provincial	confidential credential essential partial potential preferential presidential spatial substantial torrential

ACTIVITIES

Endings which sound like /shul/ (1)

This activity follows the vowel or consonant rule for adding -cial/-tial.

Endings which sound like /shul (2)

A reversal of the above activity, where children are asked to recognise the misspellings.

EXTENSION

Children may wish to try to include these /shul/ spellings in a One-Word-Story. Working with a partner or within a small group, children contribute one word each to construct a story. Children receive points for including a /shul/ word, providing that it is in context and they are able to spell it correctly.

ACTIVITY

Endings which sound like /shul/ (1)

The sheep have a problem! They need to add some /shul/ endings onto these words, but should it be -cial or -tial?

Eggstein has a solution!

Listen to the sound before the /shul/. If it's a vowel, add -cial; if it's a consonant, add -tial.

_____   _____

_____   _____

_____   _____

_____   _____

_____   _____

-cial

-tial

Cut out the start of these words. Add them to the correct pile, then write in the ending.

spe	presiden	essen	benefi
par	substan	offi	confiden
artifi	cru	gla	so

10

© Badger Learning

Endings which sound like /shul/ (2)

The ducks have been told they can splat the misspelt words. Give them a hand!

official	sequential	special	racial
offitial	sequencial	spetial	ratial
superficial	benefitial	potencial	presidential
superfitial	beneficial	potential	presidencial
crucial	confidential	essencial	social
crutial	confidencial	essential	sotial
fatial	martial	influential	torrencial
facial	marcial	influencial	torrential

Don't forget, -cial is used after a vowel and -tial is used after a consonant.

© Badger Learning

11

Words ending in -ant, -ance/-ancy, -ent, -ence/-ency

Rules and guidelines*

Words ending in -ant, -ance/ -ancy; -ent, -ence/-ency	Use **-ant** and **-ance/-ancy** if there is a related word with a clear /a/ or /ai/ sound in the right position (**-ation** endings are often a clue). Use **-ent** and **-ence/-ency** after soft **c** (/s/ sound), soft **g** (/j/ sound) and **qu**, or if there is a related word with a clear /e/ sound in the right position. There are many words, however, where the above guidelines don't help. These words just have to be learnt.	observant, observance (observation), expectant (expectation), hesitant, hesitancy (hesitation), tolerant, tolerance (toleration), substance (substantial), innocent, innocence, decent, decency, frequent, frequency, confident, confidence (confidential), assistant, assistance, obedient, obedience, independent, independence.

Additional information

Numerous authorities offer partial rules for these suffixes, but then identify such a quantity of exceptions as to make them practically redundant. However, given that children will be working within a limited vocabulary, some guidance can be given.

Add -ant/-ance/-ancy when:	Examples	Add -ent/-ence/-ency when:	Examples
Root ends in hard c or g	applicant arrogant	Root ends in soft c or g	innocent urgent
Root word ends in y (change y to i)	reliant defiant	Root ends in short i /i/+d	confidence evident

Most words ending in -erence will follow a letter f, e.g. difference, interference, circumference. Exceptions are coherence and reverence (e is retained from root words cohere and revere), belligerence and sufferance.

-ant and its forms are also more likely to follow a recognisable root verb, e.g. hesitate becomes hesitant, whereas the verb to which -ent and its forms have been attached will be less obvious, e.g. obedient.

When the word is an occupation or agent, the word is more likely to be spelt -ant, e.g. accountant, servant, occupant, but exceptions exist, e.g. president, resident.

It may also be possible to find the correct spelling of a word ending with the -ant/-ent suffix by adding -tial to change the syllable stress, hence evidence becomes evidential and finance becomes financial.

ACTIVITIES

Words ending in –ant, –ance/ –ancy, –ent, –ence/–ency (1)

This activity responds to the soft c/g : hard c/g rule, asking pupils to identify misspellings. It relies on pupils' orthographic memory and ability to read the words. Less able children may need help within a focus group.

Words ending in –ant, –ance/ –ancy, –ent, –ence/–ency (2)

This activity encourages pupils to recognise word families and to identify that -an and -en spelling patterns are consistent. Two examples link three words (hesitant, hesitance, hesitancy; dependent, dependence, dependency).

Words ending in –ant, –ance/ –ancy, –ent, –ence/–ency (3)

In this activity two rules are addressed at one time. Children are asked to complete the words correctly and find the root word.

Words ending in –ant, –ance/ –ancy, –ent, –ence/–ency (4)

This activity relates -ance and -ence endings to their related /shul/ words. The activity is printed twice on this sheet to reduce photocopying.

Words ending in –ant, –ance/ –ancy, –ent, –ence/–ency (5) (2 versions)

Demonstrates the -erence/-erance rule. Children write their findings on the bottom of the page. The first sheet gives the initial part of the rule for pupils to complete; in the second, for more able pupils, the board is blank.

EXTENSION

Can pupils find more words that exist in these three forms,? Which words only use -ance/-ence and which -ancy/-ency?

EXTENSION

How many words can the children find which end in 'iance' or 'dence'?

EXTENSION

Can children find other /shul/ words? Does the change in syllable stress help them to find the correct -ence/-ance ending?

Words ending in -ant, -ance/-ancy, -ent, -ence/-ency (1)

-ant or -ent?

There's been a batch of dodgy words! Chris has asked Rooter and Tooter to root out all of the incorrect words. Highlight the mistakes, then rewrite the words properly on William's cart.

A c or g before an -ant ending always makes a hard sound like cat or gap. A c or g before an -ent ending always makes a soft sound like cell or germ.

magnificant   extravagent   fluorescent   complacent   intelligant

arrogent   innocent   indulgant   reminiscant   detergent

crescent   adjacent   applicant   significent   negligent

vacant   urgant   elegent   accent   agant

13

ACTIVITY

Words ending in -ant, -ance/-ancy, -ent, -ence/-ency (2)
-ant to -ance/-ancy; -ent to -ence/-ency?

The Chicken Pickers have to move faster so they're trying skates. They must find the words that fit together as families. Can you draw the paths they have to take?

pregnancy

relevant   dependence   absorbency

decent

pregnant   hesitance   fluency

important

absorbent   significance

vacant   agency

current   relevance

fluent   vacancy

agent   violence

dependent   currency

elegant   absence

absent   dependency

significant   importance

patient   hesitancy

hesitant   elegance

violent   decency

patience

Write the word families down here as you find them.

_____

_____

_____

14   © Badger Learning

Words ending in -ant, -ance/-ancy; -ent, -ence/-ency (3)
-ance or -ence?

Chris has just got an order for some -ance and -ence words. Baabara's too busy rocking out so Martha's in charge! Chris gives Martha some very clear instructions.

> If the root word ends in y, change y to i then add -ance.
> If the root ends with a short i + d (rhymes with hid), add -ence.

It'll never work: Martha's head is too full of turnips! Write the correct word for her, and then see if you can work out the root word – if there is one!

defi	defiance
Root word	defy

resid	
Root word	reside

confid	
Root word	

appli	
Root word	

reli	
Root word	

provid	
Root word	

coincid	
Root word	

compli	
Root word	

vari	
Root word	

evid	
Root word	

Words ending in -ant, -ance/-ancy; -ent, -ence/-ency (4)
-ance or -ence?

If you're still not sure whether to use -ance or -ence, try saying the word with a /shul/ ending.

essance or essence

Say ess**a**ntial and ess**e**ntial. Which sounds right?

finance or finence

Say fin**a**ncial and fin**e**ncial. Which sounds right?

substance or substence

Say subst**a**ntial and subst**e**ntial. Which sounds right?

residance or residence

Say resid**a**ntial and resid**e**ntial. Which sounds right?

Words ending in -ant, -ance/-ancy; -ent, -ence/-ency (4)
-ance and -ence

If you're still not sure whether to use -ance or -ence, try saying the word with a /shul/ ending.

essance or essence

Say ess**a**ntial and ess**e**ntial. Which sounds right?

finance or finence

Say fin**a**ncial and fin**e**ncial. Which sounds right?

substance or substence

Say subst**a**ntial and subst**e**ntial. Which sounds right?

residance or residence

Say resid**a**ntial and resid**e**ntial. Which sounds right?

Words ending in -ant, -ance/-ancy; -ent, -ence/-ency (5)
-erence or -erance?

More word destruction! Put a duck Karate chop to show where the -erence/-erance letters join these words.

Circle the letter that comes before the letter string.

Can you finish writing Eggstein's rules?

interf(e)rence   perseverance

circumference   conference

inference   tolerance

deliverance   difference

preference   exuberance

utterance   furtherance

Rules for -erence and -erance

If there's a letter f, add

_____ .

If there isn't a letter f, add

_____ .

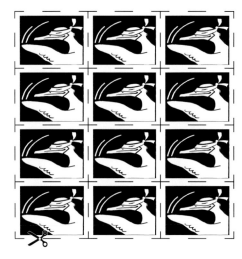

Words ending in -ant, -ance/-ancy; -ent, -ence/-ency (5)
-erence or -erance?

More word destruction! Put a duck Karate chop to show where the erence/erance letters join these words.

Circle the letter that comes before the letter string.

Can you write some rules for adding -erence and -erance on Eggstein's board?

interf(f)erence   perseverance

circumference   conference

inference   tolerance

deliverance   difference

preference   exuberance

utterance   furtherance

```
┌─────────────────────────────┐
│   Rules for -erence and      │
│          -erance             │
│                              │
│   _____ .      │
│                              │
│   _____ .      │
│                              │
│   _____ .      │
│                              │
│   _____ .      │
└─────────────────────────────┘
```

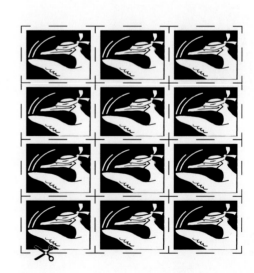

18

Words ending in -able and -ible

Rules and guidelines*

Words ending in -able and -ible	The -able ending is far more common than the -ible ending. As with -ant and -ance/-ancy, the -able ending is used if there is a related word ending in -ation. If the -able ending is added to a word ending in -ce or -ge, the e after the c or g must be kept, as those letters would otherwise have their 'hard' sounds (as in *cap* and *gap*) before the a of the -able ending. The -able ending is usually, but not always, used if a complete root word can be heard before it, even if there is no related word ending in -ation. The first six examples opposite are obvious; in *reliable*, the complete word *rely* is heard, but the y changes to i in accordance with the rule. The -ible ending is common if a complete root word can't be heard before it, but it also sometimes occurs when a complete word *can* be heard (e.g. sensible)	adorable (adoration), applicable (application), considerable (consideration), tolerable (toleration), changeable, noticeable, forcible, legible, dependable, comfortable, understandable, reasonable, enjoyable, reliable, possible, horrible, terrible, visible, incredible, sensible.

Additional information

The first piece of guidance states, 'The -able ending is far more common than the -ible ending'. A quick search using the morewords site (www.morewords.com) lists 1478 -able words and 219 -ible words, which represents a ratio of almost 7:1. While this does not take into consideration appropriate vocabulary, or exclude words where the letter strings are not used as a suffix, it remains clear that pupils would be well advised to opt for an -able ending if they are uncertain of the spelling of a word. As a caveat, this ratio plummets to 1:1 when considering words with a -sible/-sable ending.

As stated in the guidelines, if a root word can be clearly heard, then it is likely that the suffix -able will be used (if the root word ends in er it will always take the -able suffix). Exceptions of root word + -ible include: accessible, collapsible, collectible, convertible, deductible, (in)destructible, (in)digestible, (in)flexible, (ir)reversible, sensible.

These words are best taught as a list.

ACTIVITIES

Words ending in -able and -ible (1)

This activity relates the -able word ending to -ation endings. Children are asked to find the root verb each time.

Words ending in -able and -ible (2)

This activity introduces multiple rules. Children should complete this sheet and use it for reference when completing the next activity.

Words ending in -able and -ible (3)

This sheet uses the rules introduced in the previous worksheet.

EXTENSION

Can the children think of -able/-ible words to fit into pairs of sentences, e.g.

The sandwich looked _____ible.
The sandwich looked _____able.

The dog was noisy and _____ible.
The dog was noisy but _____able.

His writing was _____ible.
His writing was _____able.

Words ending in -able and -ible (1)

Is it -able or -ible?
If a word ends in -ation, it will usually also have an -able ending. Cross off the -ation endings and add -able

-ation word	Knock off the -ation	Add -able	Can you find the root verb?
admiration	admir	admirable	admire
observation			
adoration			
application			
separation			
inflammation			
consideration			
appreciation			
demonstration			
expectation			
navigation			
consolation			

ACTIVITY

Words ending in -able and -ible (2)

Look at Eggstein's Handy Hints, then add -able or -ible to the words.

Eggstein's handy hints!

If a consonant is followed by y,
change y to i before adding -able.

If a word ends in ce or ge,
keep the e when adding -able.

If a word ends in ce,
drop the e when adding -ible
No words end in -ceible or -geible

---

envy   enviable

justify   _____

vary   _____

ply   _____

deny   _____

identify   _____

replace   replaceable

service   _____

peace   _____

knowledge   _____

manage   _____

change   _____

force   forcible

produce   _____

reduce   _____

*There aren't many
words ending in ce that have
an -ible ending!*

ACTIVITY

Eggstein's handy hint!

If the root is a real word, add -able (but take care with words ending in e and y).
If the root is not a real word, add -ible.

I don't know whether to dribble or drabble the ball!

Add -able or -ible to these words:

accept_____	divis_____	laugh_____
incred_____	fashion_____	remove_____
comfort_____	imposs_____	measure_____
manage_____	achieve_____	horr_____
prevent_____	invis_____	adapt_____
reason_____	illeg_____	adjust_____
compat_____	rely_____	enjoy_____
invinc_____	notice_____	compare_____

Circle all the words that end in -ible.

Adding suffixes beginning with vowels to words ending in -fer

Rules and guidelines*

Adding suffixes beginning with vowels to words ending in -fer	The **r** is doubled if the **-fer** is still stressed when the ending is added. The **r** is not doubled if the **-fer** is no longer stressed.	referring, referred, referral, preferring, preferred, transferring, transferred, reference, referee, preference, transference	prefer

Additional information

The rule is limited to very few root words: confer, defer, differ, infer, offer, prefer, refer and transfer.

As you can see in the table below, only the words 'differ' and 'offer' retain a single r when adding the suffixes -ed and -ing. These words have a syllable stress on the first syllable in their root word. In contrast, all of the words retain a single r when adding the suffix -ence as the stress moves to the first syllable.

Root word	+ed	+ing	+ence	+al	+ able	+ ee
con**fer**	con**fer**red	con**fer**ring	*con**fer**ence*	con**fer**ral		
de**fer**	de**fer**red	de**fer**ring	*de**fer**ence*	de**fer**ral	de**fer**rable	
differ	*differed*	*differing*	*difference*			
in**fer**	in**fer**red	in**fer**ring	*in**fer**ence*			
offer	*offered*	*offering*				
pre**fer**	pre**fer**red	pre**fer**ring	*pre**fer**ence*		*pre**fer**able*	
re**fer**	re**fer**red	re**fer**ring	*re**fer**ence*	re**fer**ral		*re**fer**ee*
trans**fer**	trans**fer**red	trans**fer**ring	*trans**fer**ence*	trans**fer**ral	trans**fer**rable	

N.B. Words which are not commonly used are omitted from this table.

ACTIVITY

Adding suffixes beginning with vowels to words ending in -fer

Due to the nature of the rule, this activity relies on the use of syllable stress. This implies a familiarity with the words used. Teachers may prefer to work through the activity as a group or class if pupils are unfamiliar with the pronunciation of these words. For children who find specific difficulty in the recognition of syllable stress, rote learning of these words may be a more appropriate option.

Adding suffixes beginning with vowels to words ending in -fer

If the -fer part of the word is stressed, then the correct spelling is -ferr; if not, then it is -fer.
Can you work out the correct spelling for each word?

Read out each word and stick a Silly Bull label above the stressed part (the bit you say loudest).

Root word	1st syllable	2nd syllable	suffix	✓ or ✗
differ	dif	fer	ed	
	dif	ferr	ed	
transfer	trans	fer	ed	
	trans	ferr	ed	
prefer	pre	fer	ed	
	pre	ferr	ed	

1st syllable	2nd syllable	suffix	✓ or ✗
dif	fer	ing	
dif	ferr	ing	
trans	fer	ing	
trans	ferr	ing	
pre	fer	ing	
pre	ferr	ing	

1st syllable	2nd syllable	suffix	✓ or ✗
dif	fer	ence	
dif	ferr	ence	
trans	fer	ence	
trans	ferr	ence	
pre	fer	ence	
pre	ferr	ence	

Using the hyphen to link words

Rules and guidelines*

Use of the hyphen to link words	Hyphens can be used to join a prefix to a root word, especially if the prefix ends in a vowel and the root word also begins with one.	e.g. co-ordinate, re-iterate, pre-eminent, co-own.

Additional information

Edward Rankin (*Spellchecker with rules*) identifies a masterful set of rules for when to use a hyphen to link words, but it would leave the majority of people reaching for their dictionaries. Hyphenating words is, it would appear, a complicated task. The rules and guidelines restrict the focus to prefixes, but even here Jane Strauss in *The Blue Book of Grammar and Punctuation* (2008: 67) identifies eight specific rules. Little wonder, then, that the official guidance is coy.

Generally, hyphens are used with prefixes when:

* the root word begins with a vowel that is also the final letter of the prefix;*
* the resultant word could be confused with an identical word, e.g. re-cover and recover;
* the prefix creates a confusion if a hyphen is not used, e.g. co-worker and do-gooder (coworker gives the impression of someone employed to 'ork' cows and, similarly, dogooder can be read as an 'ooder' of dogs!)

*An exception occurs with the vowel o which is often, but not always, optional in this matter; co-operate and cooperate are both acceptable, whereas co-own is always hyphenated. British English tends towards more hyphenation than American English, but less commonly occurring words are always hyphenated. For the purposes of simplicity, the rule of double vowels is extended to the prefix co-.

The appearance of a hyphen in 'reiterate' in the example words is surprising as the *Concise Oxford English Dictionary* (a relatively conservative source) offers the following advice:

'Words formed with re- tend to be unhyphenated: restore, reacquaint. An exception to this occurs when the word to which re- attaches begins with e, in which case a hyphen is often inserted for clarity: re-examine, re-enter... Similar guidelines apply to other prefixes, such as pre-.'

© 2008 Oxford University Press

ACTIVITY

Using a hyphen to link words

This activity consists of rewriting the root words with a prefix.

EXTENSION

Children find more examples of hyphenated words and identify how many use prefixes. Is a standard rule always followed? If not, then why?

Using a hyphen to link words

Rooter and Tooter have found some hyphens. Write out these words, joining the prefix to the root. You only need to use a rootin'–tootin' hyphen when two of the same vowel are next to each other.

Write out your hyphenated words underneath each row:

semi	final	tone	automatic	circle

_____

_____

pre	assemble	exist	eminent	occupied

_____

_____

re	apply	employ	invent	view

_____

_____

re	evaluate	adjust	edit	estimate

_____

_____

co	operate	ordinate	incidence	exist

_____

_____

Words with the /ee/ sound spelt ei after c

Rules and guidelines*

Words with the /ee/ sound spelt ei after c	The 'i before e except after c' rule applies to words where the sound spelt by ei is a clear /ee/. **Exceptions**: protein, caffeine, seize	deceive, conceive, receive, perceive, ceiling (+ deceit, conceit, receipt).

Additional information

The 'i before e except after c' rule becomes rather less helpful when one considers this from a child's perspective.

The problem lies in recognising when the rule is applicable. The /see/ sound can be produced in many different ways:

- s followed by e – secret, sequel;
- s followed by ea – seat, sealant;
- s followed by ee – seen, seeking;
- s followed by ie – siege;
- s followed by ei – seize;
- sc followed by e – scene, scenery;
- c followed by e – cedar;
- c followed by ea – cease;
- c followed by ei – ceiling, receive;
- c followed by ie – policies, fancied, etc.

The ei vowel pair can also make a variety of sounds. In the words 'weight', 'weird', 'height', 'forfeit', and 'their', the vowel pair creates a different phoneme.

What we can say is that in reading:

- a 'cei' combination will always (within the constraints of reasonable vocabulary) create a /see/ sound;

  ... and in spelling:

- an /ee/ sound after c is usually 'cei' if it is at the start or in the middle of a word (exceptions are forms of 'cease' and 'conceal', the variants of the words 'exceed', 'proceed', 'succeed' and a few 'e consonant e' words, e.g. 'concede', 'recede').

Thus, the rule only becomes helpful when the child is aware that the letter c is to be used and the following sound is /ee/.

ACTIVITIES

Words with ei and ie

Children are asked to cut out the words (or simply reference them if preferred) and use the sorting structure to separate them into categories. Once completed, this is intended to provide a discussion point for when ei is said as /ee/ and when it is not. Children are directed to find that the /ee/ sound after c as /s/ can also be made by -cie at the end of words.

Words with ei and ie (continued)

The second activity uses the ei after c as /s/ category to prompt children in spelling all of the cei words correctly. All words used on this sheet will have been sorted in the previous activity.

EXTENSION

Give children sets of individual letters and ei/ie cards. How many words can they make within a set time?

Words with ei and ie

Eggstein's amazing word sorter!

Start with the word at the top of the ramp and see which box it goes to.

Is the i before e?

Is ei after c as /s/?

Is ie after c as /s/?

Yes

No

ei after c as /s/

ei but not after c as /s/

ie after c as /s/

ie but not after c as /s/

Glue these words onto the next page

sieve	friend
efficient	weight
their	perceive
policies	leisure
vacancies	piece
receipt	ceiling
height	emergencies
deceive	agencies
currencies	retrieve
receive	foreign

Words with ie and ei (continued)

Write the rule for ei after c as /s/ on Eggstein's board.

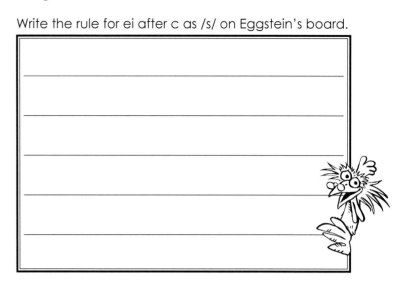

Put all the words with
ei after c as /s/
here.

Write ei or ie into these words.

fr____nd   s____ve   rec____ve

w____ght   c____ling   retr____ve

l____sure   rec____pt   h____ght

p____ce   dec____ve   th____r

The next lot are
new words. If you're
not sure how to spell them,
use a dictionary
to help.

prot____n   s____ze   caff____ne

What do
you notice about
the spelling and the
vowel sound of
these words?

Words containing the letter-string -ough

Rules and guidelines*

Words containing the letter-string ough	ough is one of the trickiest spellings in English – it can be used to spell a number of different sounds.	ought, bought, thought, nought; rough, tough, enough; cough; though, although, dough; through; thorough, borough; plough	

Additional information

As stated in the Rules and guidelines, ough is a tricky letter string, but it is at least reliably tricky and, given its multitude of pronunciations, it seems possessed of a certain subversive quality that has a peculiar fascination. Boyd (1961:189), while suggesting spelling reform, also lamented the potential extinction of this 'most characterful set of forms'. There is, not withstanding its personal attraction, no helpful way to teach children when to use the letter string, other than to recognise and learn the words!

The eight different sounds likely to be encountered by this age range are given below.

/ow/	/oh/	/oo/	/off/	/or/	/uff/	/up/	/uh/
plough	although	through	cough	bought	enough	hiccough	borough
drought	dough		trough	nought	rough		thorough
bough	though			ought	tough		
				thought			
				fought			
				sought			

As you can see, ough followed by t produces the sound /ort/.

ACTIVITIES

Words containing the letter-string ough (1), and (1) continued

The first sheet contains columns of letters for the children to cut out and place side by side. The columns can be repositioned to create different ough words. The second sheet uses these materials as the resource for a code game.

Words containing the letter-string ough (2)

This is a simple sorting activity, revealing that the ough letter-string can be used for a variety of sounds.

EXTENSION

Offer the children the following challenge:

Add a letter in each gap to make the words make sense.

1 ough_   _ ough _   _ _ ough_
(ought, bought, brought)

2 _ough,   _ _ough,   _ _ _ough,
_ _ _ _ ough
(tough, though, through, thorough)

Words containing the letter-string ough (1) continued on next page

Martha's confused… again! She has been asked to use these letters and the letter string ough to put together some words ready for fixing. The word pieces have even been numbered to help her.

On your sheet, follow the 'number code' for each letter position to make ough words.

☐ means there's no letter in this position in the word.

Example: First position	Second position		Final position	Word
2 = b	2 = r	ough	2 = t	brought

First position	Second position			Final position
1 ☐	1 ☐			1 ☐
2 b	2 r	**ough**		2 t
3 e	3 n			3 out
4 w	4 l			
5 d				
6 th				
7 p				
8 t				
9 f				
10 s				
11 l				
12 c				
13 r				
14 n				

Breaking the code: if there's a 2 in the first letter position, look at number 2 in the First position list - it's a b. Write b as the first letter of your word. Do the same to find the other letters.

Words containing the letter-string ough (1) continued

2	1	ough	2	word
b	□		t	bought

3	3		□	word

2	2		2	word

6	2		□	word

7	4		□	word

Use these empty boxes to find more ough words.
You could put number codes in to set words for a partner to guess,

		ough	
		ough	

Write your new ough words here.

_____

_____

Words containing the letter-string ough (2)

Rhyming words

Can you find ough words that rhyme with:

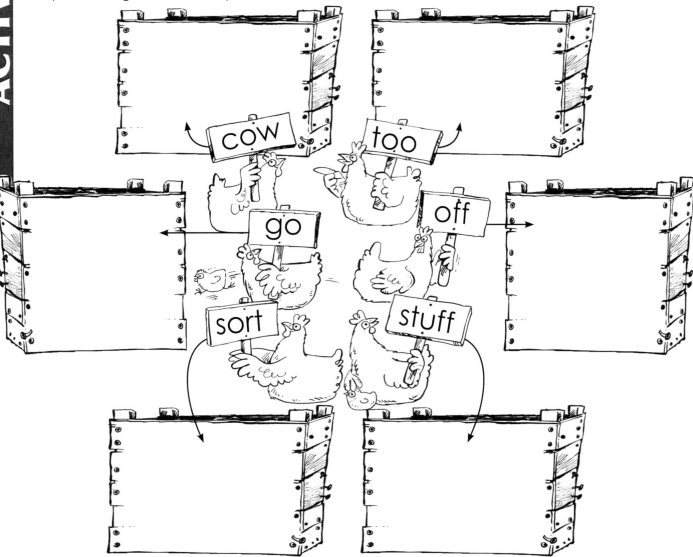

What other sounds can ough make? Write the words here.

_____

_____

_____

enough	although	trough	plough	nought
thought	fought	tough	dough	thorough
cough	drought	bought	rough	
brought	bough	though	through	

Words with 'silent' letters
(letters which cannot be predicted from the pronunciation of the word)

Rules and guidelines*

Words with 'silent' letters (letters which cannot be predicted from the pronunciation of the word)	Some letters which are no longer sounded used to be sounded hundreds of years ago: e.g. in *knight,* the **k** was sounded as /k/ and the **gh** used to represent the sound that 'ch' now represents in the Scottish word *loch.*	doubt, island, lamb, solemn, thistle, knight.

Additional information

Carney (1994: 40) identifies different types of silent letters:

- auxiliary letters cannot be heard, but they do influence the word; the u following g in guard and guide ensures that the g remains guttural;

- inert letters are those which are silent in some forms yet become active within others, examples include: sign and signature; bomb and bombard; solemn and solemnity;

- Empty letters remain silent in all forms, examples include: answer, knight, lamb, island, honest.

Background

Silent letters are present due to a word's etymology. In some instances, the silent letter would once have been pronounced, e.g. /k/ nee, but in other instances the letter was silent in its original form, e.g. hour. Throughout the centuries, silent letters were inserted in sometimes mistaken attempts to reflect a word's origin; the words island, doubt and scent are examples. For some speakers, a letter becomes silent due to elision or vowel smoothing; this may be due to personal habit or regional accent.

The process works in the opposite direction, too. As more of the population became literate, there was a move towards spelling pronunciations which became the norm for some words: the letter h, originally silent in 'hospital', is always pronounced and it is now unusual to hear the word 'hotel' pronounced without the initial /h/. The word 'often' is increasingly pronounced with a /t/, yet the word 'soften' is not. As far back as 1926, in his *Dictionary of Modern English Usage,* Fowler comments, 'No effort should be made to pronounce the t …But some good people, afraid they may be suspected of not knowing how to spell, say the t in self-defence.'

Teaching

For whatever reason a letter is silent in a child's speech, it is likely to pose a difficulty when they try to spell the word. Some children may benefit from (mentally) voicing the silent letter, while those with a strong orthographic memory may be able to identify inert letters by considering word families.

Letter pairings are common for silent letters, they include:

Letter position	Letter pair	Examples	Notes
start	kn pronounced as /n/	knot, knight	The k was once pronounced..
	gu pronounced as /g/	guest, guide	The u separates the g from a vowel to retain hard /g/ rather than soft /j/.
	wr pronounced as /r/	wrist, wrench	From Old English – the w ceased to be pronounced c.1450 – 1700 (www.etymonline.com).
	wh pronounced as /h/	who, whole	Some accents will aspirate the wh in some words.
middle	dj pronounced as /j/	adjective, adjust	
	nd pronounced as /n/	handkerchief	Silence is due to elision in compound words.
	st pronounced as /s/	listen, castle	
	ft pronounced as /f/	soften, often	Some accents will pronounce the t.
end	mb pronounced as /m/	comb, climb	some inert (e.g. bomb); some empty (e.g. comb)
	mn pronounced as /m/	column, solemn	
at various points	gn pronounced as /n/	gnaw, sign	The gn at the start of words is from a different form.
	gh	ghost, aghast, high	The gh at the start of words is from a different origin to that at the end of words.
	sc pronounced as /s/	scissors, muscle	from Latin (or assumed to be from Latin).
	sw	sword, answer	

ACTIVITIES

Words with silent letters (1)

All of the words given have silent letters occurring within the first pair (wr, gh, gu, kn, gn).

Words with silent letters (2)

This sheet uses silent letter pairs from the first activity. Teachers may wish children to write out the words with the silent letter in place, cut out the words and insert the silent letter or compile categories of silent letters. Some words (now, rite, night) are correct spellings in their own right.

EXTENSION

How many more words can the children find where the removal of a silent letter creates a new word?

Words with silent letters (3) and (4)

A repeat of the first two activities where silent letters occur in the middle (st, tg) or at the end of words (gn, mb, mn).

Words with silent letters (5)

A simple sorting activity. Words without silent letters have been selected for strong grapheme/phoneme correspondence. The activity introduces some different silent letter pairings (pn, sc, bt, ui, ps), but it is anticipated that (with the exception of the word pneumonia) all words will be familiar to the children.

Words with silent letters (6)

This activity places a focus on the use of word families to identify inert letters. The words 'bomb' and 'sign' have been chosen as they have a greater number of cognates in comparison to other words containing inert letters. Teachers may wish children to refer to dictionaries for this activity.

EXTENSION

Can children find the inert letters in other words from cognates, e.g. solemnity – solemn; autumnal – autumn; condemnation – condemn?

ACTIVITY

Words with 'silent' letters (1)

Can you find and colour the silent letters in these words?

wrong

wrinkle

wrench

wrap

guest

knot

ghost

knead

gnash

wreck

knife

knock

guide

wriggle

guilt

36

© Badger Learning

Words with 'silent' letters (2)

Can you work out which letters are missing in these words?

rist

gastly

garantee

gardian

now

naw

goul

gard

gitar

getto

rite

gess

night

nome

restle

nee

ACTIVITY

Words with 'silent' letters (3)

Can you find and colour the silent letters in these words?

thumb

resign

mortgage

solemn

bustle

benign

numb

climb

rustle

crumb

condemn

design

nestle

fasten

Words with 'silent' letters (4)

Can you work out which letters are missing in these words?

forein

com

bom

lim

colum

casle

glisen

autum

hym

desin

campain

grisle

lisen

Words with silent letters (5)

Help Rooter and Tooter to sort through these words.

Cut them out and give Rooter the words with silent letters; Tooter prefers the noisy ones!

NOISY

SILENT

doubt	castle	elephant	answer	reign
carpenter	shower	animal	acrobat	begin
ghost	crystal	pneumonia	thistle	debt
string	psychic	paper	muscle	calculator
thunder	pencil	scissors	perfect	biscuit

40

Words with 'silent' letters (6)

How many words can you find that have 'bomb' or 'sign' in them?

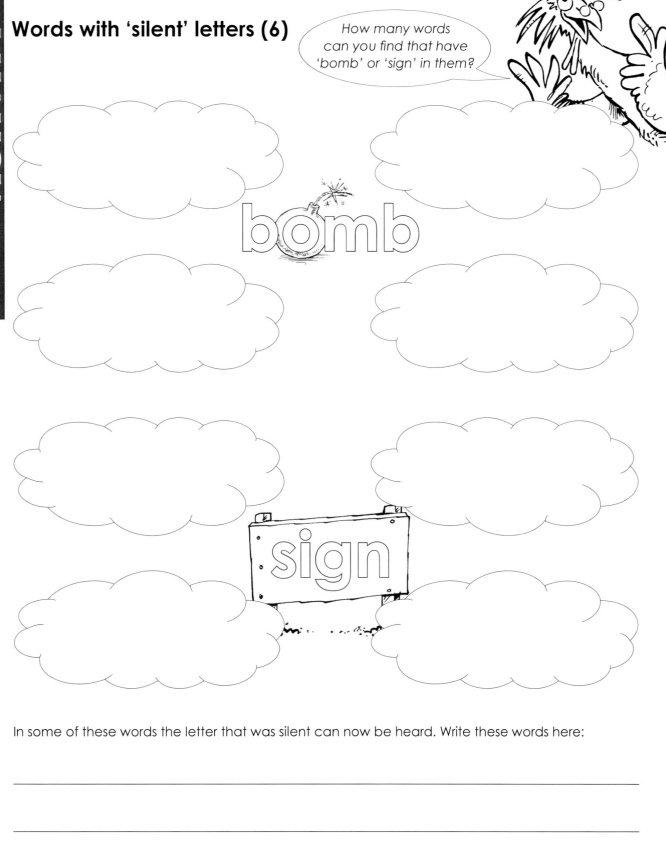

In some of these words the letter that was silent can now be heard. Write these words here:

_____

_____

_____

_____

_____

Homophones and other words that are often confused

Rules and guidelines*

Homophones and other words that are often confused	In these pairs of words, nouns end **-ce** and verbs end **-se**. Advice and advise provide a useful clue as the word advise (verb) is pronounced with a /z/ sound – which could not be spelt **c**.	advice/advise; device/devise; licence/license; practice/practise; prophecy/prophesy.

Additional information

Given that a large percentage of spelling errors arise from the selection of graphemes that could match the phoneme (e.g. 'coff' instead of 'cough'), it is hardly surprising that some children and adults are bewildered by homophones. The confusion may extend to adults' speech; one is treated to phrases such as 'the Specific (Pacific) Ocean', 'the prostrate (prostate) gland' and 'she's losing her facilities (faculties)'.

In speech, the moment is fleeting and gone. Written mistakes are more evident. Carney (1994: 81) relates: 'My local greengrocer advertises <naval oranges>, printed on a glossy trade poster. When challenged, he asserts that this is the trade spelling.' Spelling a homophone provides the double challenge of finding the correct spelling and applying it in the correct context.

The -ce (nouns)/-se (verbs) rule stated in Rules and guidelines is useful as it can be applied to a group of homophones. Other homophones simply have to be learnt individually. The phrase 'other words that are often confused' is a catch-all phrase, as confusion is likely to be an individual trait, best managed at an individual level.

ACTIVITIES

Homophones (1)
The activity focuses on the -se verb/-ce noun rule. Children sort words into verbs and nouns and use the words to complete the sentences.

Homophones (2) – whose/who's and its/it's
A resource sheet for this activity is provided on page 44. These words are taught as a unit for the purposes of analogy. Generally, once children have understood the its/it's rule they are able to extend this to whose/who's.

Homophones (3) – verb and noun pairs
A resource sheet of common verb homophones. These can be used in a variety of ways: to sort into nouns and verbs then find matching pairs; to play the memory game Pairs; as a resource sheet for writing sentences.

Homophones – example words (1) and (2)

A list of homophones and often-confused words (placed at the end of Sheet 2) from the draft curriculum. Pupils can use them to complete teacher-guided exercises, e.g. recording definitions; writing appropriate sentences.

Homophones word scramble (1) and (2)

Pairs of homophones with their letters scrambled (Sheet 1 gives the letters, Sheet 2 – for more able students – omits them). Unscrambling will reveal a hidden word. Children can create homophone anagrams for others to solve.

Homophone crossword (2 sheets)
This crossword gives links to the homophone pairs within the clues section. Note: the clues are on a separate sheet.

Homophones word search

Children are asked to find and match the homophone words. All words are spelt left to right or from top to bottom, but may be placed diagonally.

Homophone jokes
Children are asked to create better puns than the ones shown. Not tricky!

EXTENSION

Can the children create their own sentences for the remaining words?

EXTENSION

Children can look for examples of these words in reading books. They may also be able to find examples of incorrect use in newspapers and advertising materials.

EXTENSION

Some pupils may be able to find the words without the homophone list (cut from bottom of sheet). Ask them to find homophones for the word search words once all fifteen words have been found.

Homophones (1) – nouns and verbs

Draw lines to put these words on the nouns or the verbs pile.

devise

prophecy

device

licence

advice

advise

practice

prophesy

license

practise

Eggstein's handy hints

The verbs end in -se or -sy.

The nouns end in -ce or -cy.

Choose the right words to finish these sentences.

Chris is very practical. He's made an amazing _____.

Eggstein needed to _____ a new machine.

The sheep needed to _____ their welding.

The sheep went to guitar _____.

whose means 'belongs to who?'

its means 'belongs to it'

who's means 'who is' or 'who has'

it's means 'it is' or 'it has'

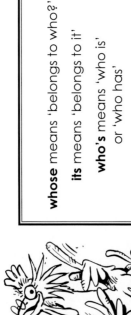

whose means 'belongs to who?'

its means 'belongs to it'

who's means 'who is' or 'who has'

it's means 'it is' or 'it has'

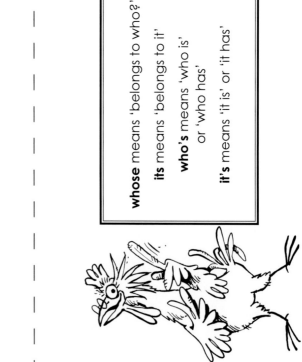

whose means 'belongs to who?'

its means 'belongs to it'

who's means 'who is' or 'who has'

it's means 'it is' or 'it has'

whose means 'belongs to who?'

its means 'belongs to it'

who's means 'who is' or 'who has'

it's means 'it is' or 'it has'

Homophones (2) – whose/who's and its/it's

Cut out the chickens. Then stick the right one for each sentence in the empty box!

They did not know _____ it was.

The dog ran after _____ ball.

"_____ coming out?"

"_____ not fair!" she shouted.

_____ is this?

_____ too late to worry!

The farm looked at _____ best.

I don't know _____ done this.

The shed lost _____ roof in the storm.

I don't know why _____ taken so long.

She knew _____ responsibility it was.

_____ been here before?

whose

whose

whose

its

its

its

who's

who's

who's

it's

it's

it's

Homophones – verb and noun pairs

caught	mist	world
board	toad	made
maid	missed	whirled
heard	thrown	towed
band	guessed	flew
herd	banned	throne
tide	coward	road
soared	rowed	tied
flu	court	guest
bored	cowered	sword

Homophones – example words (1)

aisle	
isle	
aloud	
allowed	
affect	
effect	
altar	
alter	
ascent	
assent	
bridal	
bridle	
cereal	
serial	
complement	
compliment	
descent	
dissent	
desert	
dessert	
draft	
draught	
farther	
father	
guessed	
guest	

Homophones – example words (2)

heard	
herd	
led	
lead	
morning	
mourning	
past	
passed	
precede	
proceed	
principal	
principle	
profit	
prophet	
stationary	
stationery	
steal	
steel	
who's	
whose	
disinterested	
uninterested	
eligible	
illegible	
eliminate	
illuminate	
wary	
weary	

Homophones word scramble (1)

Can you unscramble these pairs of homophones?

| Grains of wheat, oats and corn (breakfast). | cleare |
| A story told in parts | aisler |

| Seven days | ewek |
| Feeble. Not strong | awek |

| Use pen or pencil to make marks. | wrad |
| A sliding compartment in furniture. | redwar |

What is the word made by the letters in the boxes?

_____

| A part of something larger. | ecepi |
| Quiet, tranquil, calm. | apcee |

| To have little money. | orop |
| Move liquid from a container. | ourp |

| A male parent | retahf |
| At a greater distance. | fherrat |

What is the word made by the letters in the boxes?

Homophones Word Scramble (2)

Can you work out these pairs of homophones?

Grains of wheat, oats and corn (often eaten for breakfast).						
A story told in parts						

Seven days				
Feeble. Not strong				

Use pen or pencil to make marks.						
A sliding compartment in furniture.						

What is the word made by the letters in the boxes?

_____

A part of something larger.					
Quiet, tranquil, calm.					

To have little money.				
Move liquid from a container.				

A male parent							
At a greater distance.							

What is the word made by the letters in the boxes?

_____

Homophone crossword

Homophone crossword clues

Across		Homophone
2	A strong place where soldiers might live.	Down 2
4	A religious song of praise.	Down 25
6	The earliest part of the day.	Across 21
8	A sandy or pebbly shore.	Across 24
9	Where materials are joined.	Down 27
12	Office supplies, such as pens and paper.	Down 12
15	A part of the body that flexes to create movement.	Down 10
16	At this moment, or the flow of electricity.	Across 26
20	To have moved across.	Down 7
21	To feel sorrow after a death.	Across 6
22	Small or unimportant.	Down 22
24	A type of tree.	Across 8
26	A small seedless raisin.	Across 16
28	The small fruit of a tree or bush.	Down 19
29	A large deer-like mammal.	Down 13
30	A female horse.	Down 23

Down		Homophone
1	The money made from a business.	Down 3
2	To have had a fight.	Across 2
3	Someone who foretells the future.	Down 1
5	A confusing pathway often built from hedges.	Down 18
7	Some time ago.	Across 20
10	A type of shellfish.	Across 15
11	A time for teaching and learning.	Down 14
12	Still, not moving.	Across 12
13	A light, creamy dessert.	Across 29
14	To make smaller.	Down 11
15	The most important.	Down 17
17	The long hair on the neck of some animals.	Down 15
18	A type of corn, often grown in the USA.	Down 5
19	To place something into the ground.	Across 28
22	A person who digs for minerals.	Across 22
23	The leader of a town or city council.	Across 30
25	The word used when talking about a man or a boy.	Across 4
27	To appear to be.	Across 9

Homophones used:

beach/beech	berry/bury	currant/current
fort/fought	him/hymn	lessen/lesson
main/mane	maize/maze	mare/mayor
miner/minor	moose/mousse	morning/mourning
muscle/mussel	passed/past	profit/prophet
seam/seem	stationary/stationery	

ACTIVITY

Homophones word search

There's been a disaster in the sorting shed! Some homophones have been dropped and the letters are all mixed up. Can you find the words that match the homophones at the bottom of the page?

c	s	s	g	e	j	g	l	t	o
o	d	i	n	u	n	r	h	w	u
u	j	e	g	i	e	g	t	d	j
r	c	n	l	h	u	s	e	e	b
s	w	i	t	a	e	w	t	i	o
e	e	a	c	d	o	d	j	g	u
c	e	n	e	l	l	k	m	h	g
w	b	w	l	i	b	e	r	t	h
d	o	a	u	s	a	v	o	u	r
t	v	b	b	o	a	r	d	e	r

birth		whether		saver	

ate		billed		toad	

border		guessed		seen	

court		side		sealing	

coarse		aloud		bow	

Words you will find in the Homophones word search:

eight	guest	allowed	course	sighed
boarder	savour	ceiling	towed	berth
scene	build	caught	weather	bough

Homophone jokes

Oh no! Terry and Crumb have found the homophones!

Why is a sore throat like a pony?

Because it's a little hoarse.

Why were people told not to whisper?

Because it wasn't aloud.

Why was the fourteenth day so tired?

Because he was still two week.

Why did the kilogram yawn and stretch?

Because it was a long weight.

These are dreadful puns! Can you think of any better jokes for them to use?

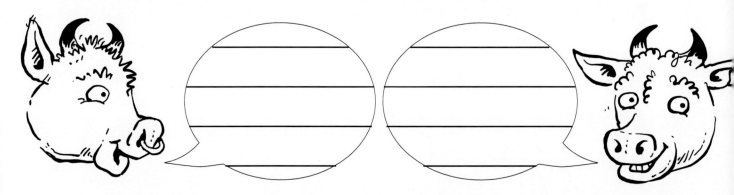

54

General resources

Word puzzles

Word chains

These are effectively Boggle© boards. Children have to find as many five-letter words as possible in each board. All words are taken from the Year 5 and 6 Word List. Words contained within the grids are listed at the bottom of the page and may be folded under when photocopying. Blank grids are provided for use by teachers or pupils to create their own boards. A very useful site for this activity is: www.hees.us/reverseboggle.cgi

Letter swap

A simple activity with two words, that rapidly grows in complexity as additional words are added. Words in the first activity are taken from this resource; words in the second activity are taken from the Year 5 and 6 Word List. Blank grids are provided for use by teachers or pupils to create their own boards.

Word squares

Children need to find as many words as possible by selecting one letter from each section of the square.

Blank sheets are provided for use by pupils.

Note: inserting letters for a few words and then adding random letters is a relatively simple task. It is significantly more challenging to ensure that letters are not repeated in each section and that there are no redundant letters.

Spelling springs

A 'learn your spellings' gimmick – but the effect of gimmicks should never be underestimated! Children should cut out the rectangle and concertina along the folds. Once spellings have been written into the spaces the first section can be glued onto the inside cover of a book. The final section incorporates tabs at either end to secure the spring. Children may wish to use the spelling spring as a ready reference or for Look/Say/Cover/Write/Check exercises. Some children may prefer to use an enlarged version of this resource sheet.

Year 5 and 6 spellings arranged by word length

Useful for puzzles and games.

Spelling list

Word Farm achievement record

Pupil record sheet to be completed and maintained by pupils.

Word chains

Make words by joining adjacent letters. How many five-letter words can you find?

1

S	E	M	C
L	Y	A	H
H	R	T	S
O	F	U	P

2

I	N	T	H
N	T	E	M
I	U	P	R
A	H	R	F

3

I	D	E	X
N	P	A	N
L	O	R	K
Q	U	E	Y

4

M	N	O	R
I	E	Q	S
P	U	Z	E
J	I	C	I

1	2	3	4
style	haunt	knead	juice
yacht	unite	rapid	equip
yeast	utter	query	minor
forty	fruit	enrol	seize
rhyme	tempt	index	
syrup	ninth		

Word chains

1

3

2

5

4

6

Letter swap (1)

The letters in these words have been swapped around. Can you sort them out?

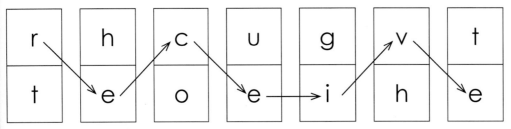

Clues: To be given something. To have been thinking something.

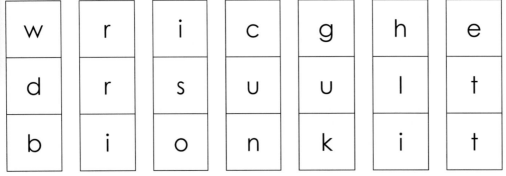

Clues: A crease on someone's face. A time when there is little or no water.
A flat, sweet treat usually sold in a packet.

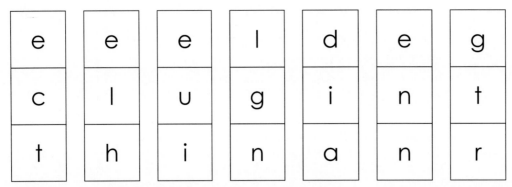

Clues: Graceful and stylish. The top surface of a room. A loud noise heard during storms.

Clues: A joint in your hand. A prickly plant with purple flowers.
Exceptional or different. To stay calm and quiet.

Letter swap (2)

The letters in these words have been swapped around. Can you sort them out?

d	r	s	t	e	o	y
p	e	o	t	r	c	t

Clues: The monster came to _____ the Earth but the superhero was able to _____ everyone!

d	u	p	g	e	a	r
s	o	c	i	l	s	l
p	e	g	u	m	a	t

Clues: 0.4 is a _____ fraction. 'I would like to _____ my own idea,' said Eggstein. Everyone likes Baarbara: she's the most _____ sheep on Word Farm.

b	l	t	v	a	f	y
f	a	a	g	o	i	r
s	a	r	i	s	u	n

Clues: The bar of chocolate was very cheap: it was a real _____ . The ice-cream had a wonderful vanilla _____ . 'Our meals are big enough to _____ the largest appetite!'

j	v	u	i	o	u	e
a	e	r	r	t	g	s
h	o	e	l	a	o	r
e	q	a	a	z	o	n

Clues: The ducks were _____ of Ninja Duck's amazing skill. The children were of _____ height. The sun dipped below the _____ . The sun shines brightly overhead at the line of the _____ .

© Badger Learning

59

Letter swap

1

2

3

4

Word squares

Start with the letter in the first square then add one letter from each surrounding square. How many words can you make?

c	h	e	c	k
o	a	u	i	n
a	i	r	l	e
c	s	n	r	m
h	d	s	t	y

p	r	e	s	e	n	t
i	e	a	y	n	x	m
c	n	r	n	t	m	d
t	k	a	f	o	r	y
u	i	l	a	e	h	g
r	i	t	s	e	c	h
e	c	s	a	b	r	t

Word squares

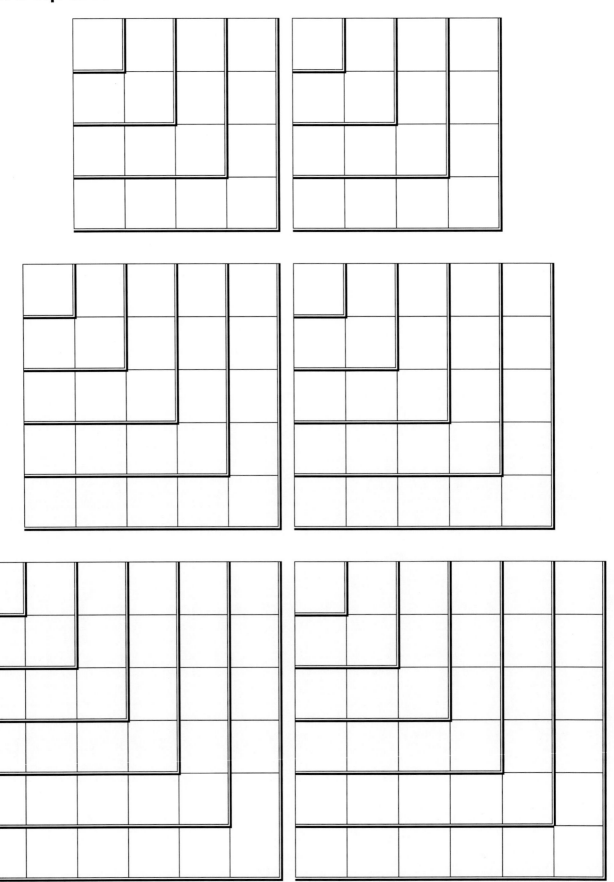

Spelling springs

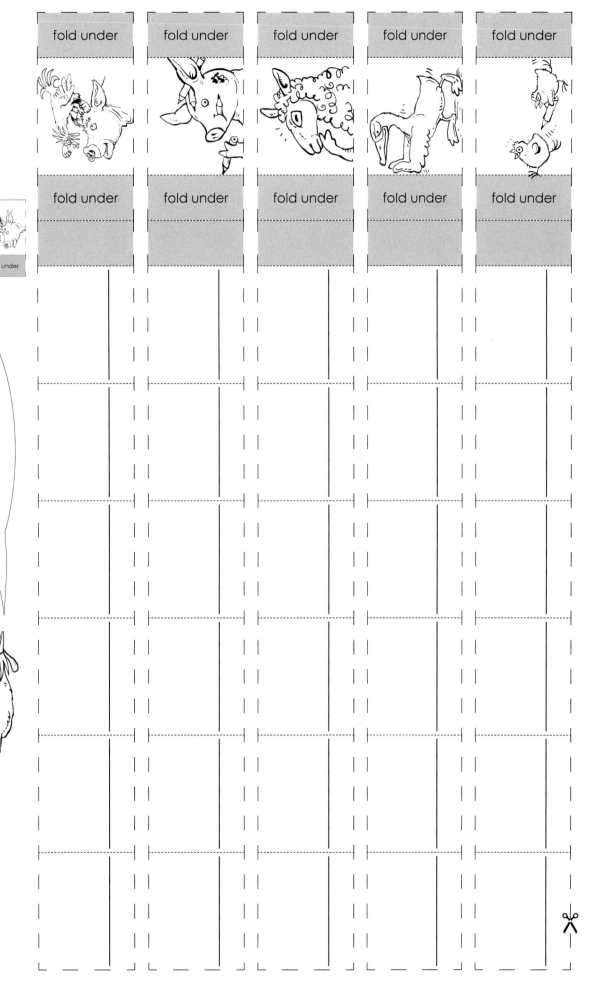

Cut out the spelling springs then write a new spelling into the spaces. Fold the paper along the dotted lines to make it springy!

fold under · fold under · fold under · fold under · fold under

fold under · fold under · fold under · fold under · fold under

fold under

Year 5 and 6 spellings arranged by word length

4
germ, hoax, jury, omit, sign, suit, vary, zero, zone — 9

5
enrol, equip, forty, fruit, haunt, index, juice, knead, minor, ninth, query, rapid, rhyme, seize, style, syrup, tempt, unite, utter, yacht, yeast — 21

6
bruise, career, coward, create, debate, endure, exceed, favour, forbid, garage, govern, harass, hearty, height, hinder, honour, lawyer, legend, length, liquid, manage, medium, modern, modest, nation, object, occupy, origin, phrase, prefer, quench, reason, recent, refuse, regret, remove, resign, revise, rhythm, scheme, severe, solemn, sphere, statue, talent, tyrant, umpire, vacant, virtue, volume, wisdom, wizard, wrench — 53

7
analyse, ancient, average, awkward, bargain, believe, blemish, century, curious, deceive, decimal, deprive, destroy, develop, equator, Europe, flavour, foreign, genuine, gradual, granite, haughty, horizon, imagine, imitate, immense, impress, include, jealous, knuckle, lecture, leisure, lenient, majesty, mineral, miracle, narrate, natural, observe, operate, opinion, popular, protect, purpose, qualify, realise, receipt, receive, request, restore, satisfy, similar, sincere, society, succeed, success, suggest, theatre, triumph, twelfth, variety, villain, volcano, whether, woollen, zoology — 66

8
apparent, attitude, boundary, convince, definite, electric, emigrate, engineer, envelope, estimate, European, evidence, excavate, familiar, festival, humility, identify, imprison, industry, inferior, junction, magazine, majority, military, mischief, moisture, mosquito, nuisance, organise, parallel, punctual, relevant, resemble, sandwich, saucepan, stubborn, superior, surprise, syllable, sympathy, thorough, tomorrow, wardrobe — 43

9
affection, celebrate, challenge, committee, embarrass, encounter, encourage, guarantee, hindrance, hurricane, influence, interfere, interrupt, interview, introduce, lightning, permanent, persevere, privilege, recommend, telescope, terminate, ventilate — 23

10
appreciate, atmosphere, correspond, especially, exaggerate, government, illustrate, inhabitant, instrument, marvellous, parliament, ridiculous, tremendous, vocabulary — 14

11
accommodate, demonstrate, explanation, investigate, manufacture, mischievous — 6

13
pronunciation — 1

Spelling list

The Word List for Year 5 and 6 from the draft curriculum comprises an impressive 236 words, listed in alphabetical order. There are numerous ways of organising this list for spelling purposes, but the range and diversity of the words frustrates simple methods of inclusive compilation. Some possible combinations are shown below

Words with silent letters

scheme, wrench, honour, knead, knuckle, yacht, rhyme, rhythm, solemn, foreign, sign, resign, length, receipt, guarantee, tempt, sandwich.*

(*depending upon accent)

ph as /f/

sphere, atmosphere, phrase, triumph.

s as /z/

reason, revise, resemble, realise, analyse, surprise, organise, observe, bruise, imprison, wisdom, resign.

ei words

(/ee/) seize, deceive, receipt, receive.

(not /ee/) height, leisure, foreign.

Double consonants relating to the first syllable

affection, apparent, appreciate, attitude, challenge, correspond, hurricane, illustrate, immense, narrate, occupy, stubborn, succeed, suggest, syllable, villain, utter, woollen.

Double consonants relating to the second syllable

exaggerate, harass, impress, interrupt, marvellous, parallel, recommend, tomorrow (especially).

Two sets of double consonants

accommodate, committee, embarrass, success.

Internet links

Note: Due to the nature of the Internet, it is vital that you check Internet links before they are used in the classroom.

www.grammarbook.com/   http://homepage.ntlworld.com/vivian.c

www.ashley-bovan.co.uk/words/partsofspeech.htm   www.spelling.hemscott.net/

www.morewords.com www.etymonline.com

Spelling games site: www.eastoftheweb.com/

Further reading

Carney, E. (1994), *A Survey of English Spelling*, London: Routledge

Cook, V. (2004), *Accomodating Brocolli in the Cemetary*, Profile Books Ltd

McLeod, M. (1961), *Rules in the teaching of spelling* in The Scottish Council for Research in Education, *Studies in Spelling*, University of London Press Ltd

Rankin, E. (1999), *Folens Spellchecker with Rules*, Folens Ltd

Word Farm achievement record

Name _____

Objective	Rules I have learnt	Achieved?
I can spell word endings which sound like /shus/ spelt –cious or –tious.		
I can spell word endings which sound like /shul/.		
I can spell words ending in –ant, -ance/-ancy, -ent, -ence/-ency.		
I can spell words ending in -ible and -able.		
I know how to add suffixes beginning with vowels to words ending in -fer.		

66

© Badger Learning

I know when to use a hyphen to link words.				
I can say the /ee/ sound spelt ei after c rule.				
I can find and spell words containing the letter-string ough.				
I can recognise and spell words with 'silent' letters.				
I know about homophones and other words that are often confused.				

Answers

Endings which sound like /shus/ spelt –cious or –tious (1) p7

ambitious	nutritious
precious	ferocious
gracious	atrocious
voracious	spacious
superstitious	infectious
vicious	cautious
fictitious	conscious

Endings which sound like /shus/ spelt –cious or –tious (2) p8

vice, malice, grace, space, avarice, office
Check children's definitions.

Endings which sound like /shul/ (1) p10

special	presidential
beneficial	essential
official	partial
artificial	substantial
crucial	confidential
glacial	
social	

Endings which sound like /shul (2) p11

Correct spellings: racial, special, sequential, official;
presidential, potential, beneficial, superficial;
social, essential, confidential, crucial;
torrential, influential, martial, facial.

Words ending in -ant, -ance/-ancy, -ent; -ence/-ency (1) -ant or -ent p13

magnificent, arrogant, extravagant, urgent, indulgent, elegant, reminiscent, significant, intelligent, agent.

Words ending in -ant, -ance/-ancy, -ent, -ence/-ency (2) -ant to -ance/-ancy -ent to -ence/-ency p14

relevant, relevance	decent, decency
pregnant, pregnancy	important, importance
absorbent, absorbency	vacant, vacancy
current, currency	fluent, fluency
agent, agency	dependent, dependence, dependency
elegant, elegance	absent, absence
significant, significance	patient, patience
hesitant, hesitance, hesitancy	violent, violence

Words ending in -ant, -ance/-ancy; -ent, -ence/-ency (3) -ance or -ence? p15

defiance – root word 'defy'
residence – root word 'reside'
confidence – root word 'confide'
appliance – root word 'apply'
reliance - root word 'rely'
providence – root word 'provide'
coincidence – root word 'coincide'
compliance - root word 'comply'
variance – root word 'vary'
evidence – no comparable root word.

Words ending in -ant, -ance/-ancy; -ent, -ence/-ency (4) -ance and -ence p16

Check children's responses.

Words ending in -ant, -ance/-ancy; -ent, -ence/-ency (5) -erence or -erance? p17

Check children's rules:
-erence follows f; -erance follows other letters.

Words ending in -able and -ible (1) p20

ation word	Knock off the ation	Add able	Can you find the root verb?
admiration	admir	admirable	admire
observation	observ	observable	observe
adoration	ador	adorable	adore
application	applic	applicable	apply
separation	separ	separable	separate
inflammation	inflamm	inflammable	inflame
consideration	consider	considerable	consider
appreciation	appreci	appreciable	appreciate
demonstration	demonstr	demonstrable	demonstrate
expectation	expect	expectable	expect
navigation	navig	navigable	navigate
consolation	consol	consolable	console

Words ending in -able and -ible (2) p21

enviable	replaceable	forcible
justifiable	serviceable	producible
variable	peaceable	reducible
pliable	knowledgeable	knowledgeable
deniable	manageable	negligible
identifiable	changeable	illegible

Words ending in -able and -ible (3) p22

acceptable	divisible	laughable
incredible	fashionable	removable
comfortable	impossible	measureable
manageable	achievable	horrible
preventable	invisible	adaptable
reasonable	illegible	adjustable
compatible	reliable	enjoyable
invincible	noticeable	comparable

Adding suffixes beginning with vowels to words ending in -fer p24

differed	differing	difference
transferred	transferring	transference
preferred	preferring	preference

Using a hyphen to link words p26

semifinal	semitone	semiautomatic	semicircle
preassemble	pre-exist	pre-eminent	preoccupied
reapply	re-employ	reinvent	review
re-evaluate	readjust	re-edit	re-estimate
co-operate (cooperate)	co-ordinate (coordinate)	coincidence	coexist

Words with ei and ie p28

weight	perceive	friend	emergencies
leisure	ceiling	piece	agencies
foreign	receipt	retrieve	policies
their	deceive	sieve	vacancies
height	receive	efficient	currencies

Words with ei and ie (continued) p29

Rule: ei after c says /see/ (or other wording)

friend	sieve	receive
weight	ceiling	retrieve
leisure	receipt	height
piece	deceive	their
protein	seize	caffeine

Words containing the letter-string ough (1) & (1) continued p31-32

bought, enough, brought, through, plough.
More ough words: Check children's responses.

Words containing the letter-string ough (2) p33

cow: plough, bough
too: through
go: although, dough, though
off: trough, cough
sort: brought, thought, fought, bought, nought
stuff: enough, tough, rough
other sounds: drought, thorough

Words with 'silent' letters (1) p36

Check children's responses.

Words with 'silent' letters (2) p37

wrist, ghastly, guarantee, know, guardian, ghoul, gnaw, guard, ghetto, guitar, gnome, guess, write, wrestle, knee, knight.

Words with 'silent' letters (3) p38

Check children's responses.

Words with 'silent' letters (4) p39

foreign, bomb, comb, column, limb, castle, glisten, autumn, design, hymn, campaign, gristle, listen.

Words with silent letters (5) p40

silent: doubt, castle, answer, reign, ghost, pneumonia, thistle, debt, psychic, muscle, scissors, biscuit.
'noisy': elephant, carpenter, shower, animal, acrobat, begin, crystal, string, paper, calculator, thunder, pencil, perfect.

Words with 'silent' letters (6) p41

bomb: bombard, bombardier, bombastic, bomber, bombing etc.
sign: design, resign, resignation, signature, signal etc.
Check the words the children wrote.

Homophones (1) p43

nouns and verbs
Nouns: device, practice, licence, advice, prophecy
Verbs: devise, practise, license, advise, prophesy
Chris made an amazing device.
Eggstein needed to devise a new machine.
The sheep needed to practise their welding.
The sheep went to guitar practice.

Homophones (2) – whose/who's and its/it's p45

They did not know whose it was.
The dog ran after its ball.
Who's coming out?
"It's not fair!" she shouted.
Whose is this?
It's too late to worry!
The farm looked at its best.
I don't know who's done this.
The shed lost its roof in the storm.
I don't know why it's taken so long.
She knew whose responsibility it was.
Who's been here before?

Homophones – verb and noun pairs p46

Check children's responses.

Homophones – example words (1) and (2) p47-48

Check children's responses.

Homophones word scramble (1) and (2) p49-50

Hidden words: reward; carpet.

Homophone crossword p51-52

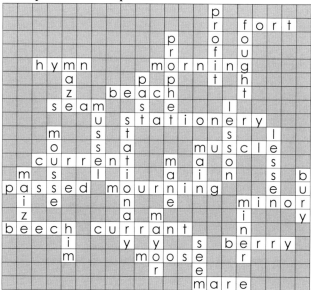

Homophones word search p53

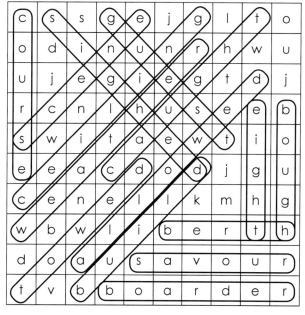

General resources: word puzzle answers

Word chains p56

Answers listed on sheet.

Letter swap (1) p58

receive	thought		
wrinkle	drought	biscuit	
thunder	ceiling	elegant	
knuckle	thistle	special	patient

Letter swap (2) p59

destroy	protect		
decimal	suggest	popular	
bargain	flavour	satisfy	
jealous	horizon	average	equator

Word squares p61

Top square: possible answers include:

check	carry	coach	coins
couch	count	court	chant
cause	coals	chain	chase
chart	coast	chins	charm
child			

Bottom square: possible answers include:

present	perfect	picking	peanuts
peasant	perfume	pressure	prayers
praying	preying	pickles	picture
pirate	pickaxe	perfuse	picnics
pickled	pertain	persons	pinnate
pennies	penalty	pennine	perform
perform	penance	perturb	persona
perkier	peckish	pickets	pretend
preying	presume	pretext	

Badger Learning
Suite G08
Business & Technology Centre
Bessemer Drive
Stevenage, Hertfordshire
SG1 2DX

Telephone: 01438 791037
Fax: 01438 791036
www.badgerlearning.co.uk

Years 5 / 6 English Sharpener: Spelling

First published 2013

ISBN 978 1 78147 080 0

Text © J.H. Rice 2013
Complete work © Badger Publishing Limited 2013

Publisher: Susan Ross
Senior Editor: Danny Pearson
Designer: Jo Digby, north & south design
Illustrator: Juliet Breese

Printed in the UK